Unless otherwise noted, Scripture passages have been taken from the Revised Standard Version, Catholic edition. Copyright ©1946, 1952, 1971 by the Division of Christian Education of the National Council of the Churches of Christ in the USA. Used by permission. All rights reserved.

Quotes are taken from the English translation of the Catechism of the Catholic Church for the United States of America (indicated as CCC), 2nd ed. Copyright ©1997 by United States Catholic Conference – Libreria Editrice Vaticana.

©2014 Life Teen, Inc. All rights reserved. No part of this book, including interior design, cover design, and/or icons, may be reproduced or transmitted in any form, by any means (electronic, photocopying, recording, or otherwise) without prior written permission from the publisher.

The information contained herein is published and produced by Life Teen, Inc. The resources and practices are in full accordance with the Roman Catholic Church. The Life Teen® name and associated logos are trademarks registered with the United States Patent and Trademark Office. Use of the Life Teen® trademarks without prior permission is forbidden. Permission may be requested by contacting Life Teen, Inc. at 480-820-7001.

Designed by David Calavitta

Authored by Mark Hart

Copy editing by Rachel Peñate

A special thanks to the Catholic youth speakers featured in "Section Three: Behind the Scenes" for their contribution to this resource.

Copyright ©2014 Life Teen, Inc. All rights reserved.
Published by Life Teen, Inc.
2222 S. Dobson Rd.
Suite 601
Mesa, AZ 85202
LifeTeen.com

Printed in the United States of America.
Printed on acid-free paper.

TABLE OF CONTENTS

Introduction...1

Section One:
Different Types of Presentations................11
    Giving a Teaching or Talk.............................13
    Offering a Testimony....................................24
    Preaching or Leading Prayer.......................29

Section Two:
Refinement..37
    Going from Good to Great............................37
    Things to be Aware of, Avoid, or Remember....41
    Ten "Dos and Don'ts" When
    Speaking to Teens..43

Section Three:
Behind the Scenes...................................53
Interviews with Several Effective Catholic Youth Speakers
    Jackie (Francois) Angel................................54
    Mary Bielski..58
    Leah Darrow...67
    Jason Evert..72
    Matt Fradd...78
    Bob Rice...83
    Chris Stefanick..87
    Joel Stepanek..93

Appendix:..103
    The Ten Commandments of
    Presenting to Teens....................................103
    A Presenter's Checklist..............................104

> "If teaching and preaching is your job, then study diligently and apply yourself to whatever is necessary for doing the job well. Be sure that you first preach by the way you live. If you do not, people will notice that you say one thing, but live otherwise, and your words will bring only cynical laughter and a derisive shake of the head."
>
> - St. Charles Borromeo

INTRODUCTION

"According to most studies, people's number one fear is public speaking. Number two is death. Death is number two. This means to the average person, if you go to a funeral, you're better off in the casket than doing the eulogy."

- Jerry Seinfeld

Years ago, the idea of speaking in front of a group – especially speaking to teenagers – scared me beyond belief. Ironically, I never wanted to be a youth minister or "speak" in front of teens. I enjoyed being the "sarcastic kid" in small group at a Life Night. I flourished in skits as the clown willing to embarrass himself. Sure, as a teen I may have lectored at Mass, but that was partially because listening to poor readers proclaim God's Word was a spiritual pet peeve. At the end of the day, I didn't mind being up front if I was acting or reading but "speaking"? Ugh, no thank you… speaking clearly was not my gift.

When I became a Core Member for the first time and my youth minister asked me to give a teaching, I almost swallowed my tongue before stupidly agreeing. I prepared for weeks; I had outlines atop outlines. I had outlines for my outlines. But, little did I realize at the time how dangerous this was… because when your number is called to give a talk, something happens in your human psyche. You think, "this is my opportunity" and you inadvertently try to cram every single thing you've ever wanted to say to a young person into one talk. You become a valedictorian on hyperdrive. All of a sudden you have so many pages of notes of wonderful theology... for a 16-year-old (who doesn't know your name, and doesn't care about you) sitting on a rag rug on a linoleum floor, in a Church hall that smells like burnt french toast.

Looking back, I had notes and had rehearsed, but *I was far from prepared*. The talk hadn't become a part of me because the presentation was all about me; my pride didn't leave any room for the Holy Spirit to fly. When it came time to give the talk, a seven minute talk went twenty-two, and to say it was awful would be a horrific understatement. It was a train wreck in every conceivable way. I took forever to make my first point. My jokes didn't work. My points got muddled. I digressed. When teens began to look disinterested I reacted with more fumbling. Teens were yawning. Core members were making faces. No one was tracking with me mentally. The youth minister was in the back of the room signaling me to stop and then pantomiming a plane crash. (Okay, not really, but in my head he did.) I lost everyone there, including myself.

After that talk, I was convinced it was a fault of my ability. I said to myself, "Well, it didn't go well, so obviously speaking is not my thing." When really, it had to do with some exterior reasons, but far more interior. My problem was not a lack of ability as much as it was a lack of perspective, of prayer, and proper preparation.

Know Your God

Whether you are comfortable or horrified at the idea of public speaking, it's okay. God doesn't care, because it isn't about you. If He chooses you, if He appoints you, then what right do you have to underestimate the power of the Holy Spirit within you? None.

You don't have to be a polished speaker, because ultimately, it's *not at all* about you.

Consider Moses as an example. He was a murderer hiding in the middle of the desert when God called him to serve... oh, and he also had a stuttering problem. Not exactly two strong building blocks for a speaker's credibility, yet God said, "This is my guy." Moses was not just an "unlikely hero," he was the unlikeliest of leaders. Have you ever wondered why God didn't just "choose" Moses' brother, Aaron, to lead the Israelites out of Egypt in the first place? After all, Aaron was a priest, and obviously, a strong speaker. Moses was a fugitive shepherd with blood on his hands. Why did God choose the "little brother" with a rap sheet in place of big brother with a resume?

God warns us, through the prophet Isaiah, about this way of thinking:

"For my thoughts are not your thoughts, neither are your ways my ways, says the Lord. For as the heavens are higher than the earth, so are my ways higher than your ways and my thoughts than your thoughts." (Isaiah 55:8-9)

And later, Christ poses this question about the 99 sheep:

"What man of you, having 100 sheep, if he has lost one of them, does not leave the 99 in the wilderness, and go after the one which is lost, until he finds it?" (Luke 15:4)

My response would be "I don't; I let one go to save the 99." Thank God I'm not God, right? The response of God is the response of perfect love: He is going to offer us salvation, even when we fail to accept it. He sees something in us that we don't see in ourselves. His love is illogical to us because it is perfect. We are so accustomed to counterfeit forms of love that when authentic love stands before us – and chases after us even when we're the ones who have gone astray – we doubt its sincerity. We also doubt our lovability and *use-ability*.

This is precisely the reason I love Moses so much. Moses was not a professional orator, yet God calls him anyway to deliver a crucial message. Go back to Exodus chapter three. What you will notice is that Moses gives God every excuse he can... "It's all about me" and God says, "It isn't about you... you *do what I command* you to do."

Moses acts like we do, in our humanity — Moses gives God excuses; God gives Moses instructions.

Have you ever said to yourself:

- I'm not comfortable speaking in front of others.
- I don't have anything to say.
- No one will listen to me.
- I'm not knowledgeable enough.
- I'm too out of touch with teens.
- Someone else would do a far better job.
- I'm too old, too overweight, too slow, too introverted, too (insert excuse here).
- I'm just too big a sinner.

Now, re-read Moses' objections to God in the third chapter of Exodus. He gives a litany of reasons why he can't fulfill the call that God has entrusted to him. God then reminds Moses that He doesn't call the equipped but, as we have all heard, He equips the called.

God knows what He is doing and why He chose you (John 15:16). Spend less time questioning why God calls you to certain things and more time rejoicing that He thinks so highly of you as to use you in the building of His Kingdom on earth.

God doesn't judge you by your insecurities, you do.

Learn From Moses: Know Yourself

We get so self-conscious, don't we? Have you ever called a friend to find out what they were wearing to a party because you were afraid to show up looking stupid? Ministry is no different; we all want to do our best for God, but are all uniquely over-aware of our sin or completely unaware of the depth of it. We are either oblivious to our unworthiness (due to our pride) or completely overwhelmed by it (due to our shame).

The devil reminds us of everything we are not in the eyes of society, but God doesn't see things that way. As St. John Paul the Great reminded us at World Youth Day in 2002, *"You are not the sum of your fears, you are the sum of the Father's love."*

Know yourself and know your insecurities. Invite God into them, and you'll get over them. The devil is going to use every insecurity against you because "when you seek to do good, evil will be at hand" (Romans 7:21). Don't be surprised when you are confronted by your insecurities, expect it. As St. Angela Merici is often quoted as saying, *"The devil doesn't sleep;*

he seeks the ruin of your soul in a thousand different ways." So every time you respond to God's call to serve and to love, realize upfront that you have an adversary... but you also have an ally in St. Michael and his angels. Pray the St. Michael prayer daily, and realize the enemy is no match for God's army.

Sure, God could've chosen smarter people to speak to your teens, but He didn't; He chose you, and He chose me. He could've chosen holier people, but He didn't; He chose you, and He chose me. The call of Moses can teach us a great deal, still today, about not only who God calls, but why He calls.

Moses was more concerned with who he wasn't than who he was. This doesn't just mean a concern about the exterior things such as what topics or talks you're good at. No, this means knowing where the devil will attack. It means knowing where the root of your insecurities lay because you have to confront those, and allow the Lord into them. *"If you are really calling me to this, I need you God. I need you to lead me. I need you to empower and teach me."*

How wonderful if we had this attitude with the Lord: before we just solve the issue, why don't we just listen to the Lord? Whatever it is, we admit those fears, we acknowledge those fears, we invite the Lord in, and then we just get over them.

Know Your Teens

There is no ideal Core Member. There is no ideal age or look. What appeals to teenagers are people who care more about them than they do about themselves. The best Core Member I've ever had was 72-years-old. At every single Life Night, she would stand at the door, look each and every teen in the eyes, speak their name, and acknowledge their presence — acknowledge their soul. She was beloved. She worked hard to give a teaching or witness, but when she stood up there, all those teens dug in, even when she stumbled, because they knew she cared about them. St. Paul reminds us, "If I speak in the tongues of men and of angels, but have not love, I am a noisy gong or a clanging cymbal. And if I have prophetic powers, and understand all mysteries and all knowledge, and if I have all faith, so as to remove mountains, but have not love, I am nothing" (1 Corinthians 13:1-2).

You could be a Fortune 500 executive, a seasoned teacher, a veteran salesperson, or a marketing guru, but when you stand before those teens, they don't care. All the training in the world cannot make up for a lack of love. They need to believe that you love them and that every word that falls from your lips is laced with a genuine concern for their authentic joy and ultimate well-being. If they don't believe you care about their soul, it doesn't matter what you say or how you say it.

Get to know the teens to whom you are being empowered to speak. Pay attention to them. Acknowledge Christ in them — that's where you earn the right to be heard. Respect of elders because of age rarely exists anymore in modern culture. A teenager will not respect you unless you respect them. They do not want to be talked down to, they do not want to be trivialized... they want it to be acknowledged that their battles are fierce, their crosses heavy, and their giants, real. Many of us have no idea how hard it is to be holy as a 16-year-old in the modern world. For most of us when we were 15 or 16 we didn't have access to so much sin... at the touch of a button... any minute of the day.

Social media, pornography, disengagement, and constant overstimulation are just a click away. They are fighting a battle that many of us have never known and would have been scarcely prepared to wage in our teenage years.

How much more important is it, then, when a teen comes to Edge, or a Life Night that you look them in the eyes, validate their presence, and say, "I am so glad that you are here"? If we understand who we are speaking to and what they need... everything we say to them will be laced with that in mind. *Never underestimate the power of an affirmation.* And that leads to the first practical "tip" in this book: If you ever are giving a talk, a witness, a homily, a teaching, and you are stuck... just affirm them. Start there. Affirmation builds a solid foundation on which to build your next point.

Words are the most powerful weapons at our disposal. Think about it — wars don't begin with missiles but with words. Marriages begin (and, sadly, end) with words. God said the word and creation spun into existence (Genesis 1:1), for "in the beginning was the Word" (John 1:1). When we, as God's children, employ words or use the Word (Scripture) to lead souls back to the eternal Word (Jesus Christ), we are acting as God acts — giving form to formlessness and life to dry bones (Ezekiel 37). Words have power... use them wisely.

SECTION ONE:
DIFFERENT TYPES OF PRESENTATIONS

In the past twenty years, I've given more talks than I can count, in more states and dioceses than I can seem to remember, and in many cities I can scarcely spell (senility is setting in). Truthfully, I think I still have yet to ever give a "great" talk. I've gotten close at times on certain occasions when I really felt the Holy Spirit moving unimpededly. Most of the time, it's a tug-of-war within myself, trying not to get in the way of God's Spirit. My spirit is willing, but my flesh is weak (Matthew 26:41). Perhaps I'm too hard on myself, perhaps not. Maybe you can relate.

So it's with that background that when I'm (frequently) asked by youth ministers and Core Members, "What are your secrets when preparing a talk for teens?" I respond, "No secrets, just the challenge to subdue myself and only let God out."

There are, to be sure, no secrets. There are tips. There are practical ideas that ensure greater effectiveness and a longer lasting message. There are communication principles that seem to hold true regardless of region, age, group, spiritual maturity level, and environmental challenges, but *there are no secrets*. The truth is that most talks fly or fail, sink or swim well before we ever open our mouths. Preparation is as important (if not more) than talk execution. I'm sure some people would disagree with me on that point, but over the years I've repeatedly found it to be true. I've watched some of the most skilled presenters in the Church today crash and burn due to lack of preparation. Likewise, I've seen some of the most self-conscious, nervous Core Members in the world – with proper preparation – give some of the most soul-challenging, life-altering talks I've ever had the pleasure of hearing.

That being said, not all talks are the same. Giving a teaching at a Confirmation class or an Edge/Life Night might seem the same, but are the teens as receptive in Confirmation class as they are at a Life Night? Probably not.

Additionally, should our preparation to offer a witness about how God has worked and is working in our lives be the same as a talk on the history of the Church? What about preaching in something like an XLT setting? Or leading prayer in a large group that precedes or follows Mass or Adoration? Certainly we wouldn't prepare the same way for those transitions as we would to give a catechetical lesson, right?

So what's the difference, and how can/should our approach vary for each?

GIVING A TEACHING OR TALK

When we offer a talk or teaching to young souls, we have the responsibility of handing on not only the literal Word of God (Scripture), but by extension, the eternal Word of God, Jesus (John 1:1). Great teachings are far more than informational; they are in*carnational*.

When we offer the Lord our bodies, voices, experiences, and skills to share His timeless truth in a timely way at this time in history, heaven rejoices. Remember, though, that we are merely called to till the soil of the teenage heart and to cast the seed of the Word. Do not let yourself fall into the trap of "needing" to see the fruit or harvest it. It could be months or years before you see fruit with certain teenagers... be patient and trust that God is working through you whether or not you see the effects of it immediately.

> "Comfort in tribulation can be secured only on the sure ground of faith holding as true the words of Scripture and the teaching of the Catholic Church."
>
> - St. Thomas More

When you offer a talk or teaching to modern teenagers, you must have a clear-cut goal. You don't have to say "everything" about a topic but you do need to *say something* about it... something memorable, practical, and above all, relevant to their teenage life. The Holy Spirit will use you to inform their minds, and the quickest and most efficient way to inform minds is to, first, transform hearts.

Preparation

In order to first construct a talk, you have to know the message. It's not about what you have to say, or about the outline. *It's about what God wants to say through you.*

The best talks are prepared over a longer period of time; the Holy Spirit is really funny in how He inspires us — He doesn't work through us according to our agenda. You cannot schedule creativity. You need to be thinking about this talk days, weeks in advance. You need something to write on at all times. I can guarantee you that the Holy Spirit is going to inspire you at the least convenient moment. In traffic... watching a movie... out on a walk. Make it a priority to remain prayerful at all times. A solid presentation begins with humility and a true desire for constant conversion and personal holiness.

Practical Steps in Constructing a Talk

1. Pray, and think about all of the main points you want to cover.
- For an Edge/ Life Night: If you have access to the outlines provided through Edge or Life Teen, utilize them as a guide and make them your own.

2. Ask yourself the following questions: How will you begin? Is there a story, analogy, verse, or something you can use to grab their attention early?
- With most modern teens you have about 45-90 seconds to gain their attention. If you can do that, they'll afford you an additional minute or two. It is a constant game of bartering, wooing, and retaining their attention.

3. Consolidate all of your notes, brainstorms, and (prayerful) insights onto one or two pages.

4. Next, begin to widdle your points down to two or three main areas (like any good high school research paper).

5. Finally, how will you end? With a prayer? A challenge? A story? All three? How can you finish strong in a way that sets up the next activity and brings glory to God, not applause to yourself?

Practice

Before you begin, acknowledge how you feel about presenting. If you are fearful, ask the Lord for strength and confidence. If you are confident, ask the Lord for humility. And always ask the Lord for wisdom, to help discern what He does and does not want shared.

1. *Know Yourself*

   a. Acknowledge any fears or anxieties you may have about presenting.

   i. Realize that the devil does *not* want you teaching about Christ's truth or leading young souls to God. He will do everything in his power to play upon your insecurities and weaknesses (Romans 7:21, 1 Peter 5:8).

   ii. The sooner you identify the areas where you are most self-conscious or susceptible to attack, invite St. Michael and your guardian angel to dwell there, praying for and defending you.

   b. Know your speaking habits.

   i. Do you walk around a lot? Do you stand still and sway? Do you talk too loud or soft?

ii. Do you overuse phrases without realizing it?
- Do you have a tendency to use "just" or "like" indiscriminately?
- Do you say "you know" or "I mean" a lot?

c. Practice the talk.

i. Give the talk in front of a camera, or record the audio.

ii. Watch it back and look for poor or distracting presentation habits.

iii. Allow a friend or family member to time you and watch you give the talk, live, with full energy. Invite them to critique it honestly.

iv. After making note of your idiosyncrasies, record/give it again but attempt to eliminate the habits.
- All of these are things you can work on in preparation and be mindful of as you present.

2. *Know Your Content*

a. Take all of that information you amassed during the talk construction stage of preparation and refine it. Remember, less is more.

i. Reduce your talk from a page of notes to a half page notecard.

ii. Next, reduce your notecard from paragraphs to sentences.

iii. Next, reduce those sentences to just key words

that signal the next point, story, or element you want to relate. Once you know your talking points (in order) so well that you need only a small card of "key words," you'll know you're ready to present your talk regardless of the distractions or anxieties that come your way.

b. If you cannot fit your information on a note card, you don't know the material well enough to present it, so practice more!

3. *Know Your Audience*

a. The more you know the audience, the more successful a presentation will obviously be, especially with teenagers. Successful talks begin long before you open your mouth.

b. Relational ministry is the key.

i. The better the relationship with a teenager, the more likely they are to listen. The more investment you've shown in their interests and lives, the more interest they will show in what you have to say.

ii. Be present as teens are arriving.
- Ask them questions about their life.
- Ask what they may need prayers for currently.
- Ask them to pray for you during your talk.
- (Each of these interactions buy you not only credibility but support.)

c. Too often we forget to ask the question *why* in our preparation for a presentation.

> *i.* Ask *why* this topic is important to you, and then ask *why* this topic would be important to a teen (or whatever audience you are speaking to).

Execution

Being prepared isn't always about just knowing what to say, it's also about being ready emotionally and physically.

Don't just pray in preparation for your talk, but have someone pray over you before you begin. Also, try to find someone, perhaps another Core Member, to prayerfully intercede on your behalf as you present.

Confront the Nerves

If you're nervous, acknowledge it and take measures to overcome it.

> *1.* Have a Core Member with whom you are close, sit right in front. So they can look at you and affirm you. Whatever you have to do to stay calm up in front, be aware of what that is, and take the measures necessary to make that happen.

> *2.* Never hold a piece of paper if you are nervous — it is too distracting. Holding the Bible is a much better idea not only as a visual reinforcement of the truth(s) you're espousing, but as a solid form of unshakeable firmness to hide shaking hands.

Be Present When You Speak

With teens, especially, it is necessary that you make eye contact. Even if it makes those in this screen-based culture uncomfortable, do it, anyway.

   1. Be relational with them. Look teens in the eyes, and greet them, affirm them, acknowledge them. Say "I'm so glad you're here" — in doing so we validate them and communicate more than just words about a topic but affirm Christ's presence within them! Ask them to pray for you. They will come back because they see Christ in you.

   2. Do not write out your entire talk, and do not read it. Even if you have notes — do not read straight from a paper unless it is a brief quote.

   3. Likewise, if you're going to quote Scripture, always have it marked *ahead of time*. There is nothing more distracting for teens than to sit and wait while a presenter "finds" the verse that was so important they had to share it but not important enough to mark the page of in their Bible.

   4. When you are presenting, remove any impediments between you and your crowd. Just moving something at a diagonal will remove the veil and put you and your audience at the same level.

   5. Watch your body movements. One idea is to divide the room into four "quadrants," and work your eye contact and movements (clockwise-or counter-clockwise) to ensure that no matter how far away you may seem physically, you are not far away emotionally. Doing this ensures that you engage each person visibly and visually.

Use Effective Visual Aids

The right visual aid gives you credibility and helps teens to focus. That being said, it has to be the "right" visual aid — one that will enhance the message rather than distract.

Our visual aids should *really* represent the Word we proclaim. There is beauty in taking teens into sacred art and icons *when they are ready*. No, most adolescent souls are not naturally prepared to appreciate the timeless beauty of iconography but that does not mean they cannot be with a little guidance. But, before a teen can behold the majesty of God in art, they have to behold the mystery of God within themselves and within the tabernacle. They have been sold counterfeit beauty for so long, that many cannot immediately appreciate or even understand authentic beauty; likewise, many cannot appreciate history, because their own history just isn't that long.

> *"I will go peaceably and firmly to the Catholic Church: for if faith is so important to our salvation, I will seek it where true faith first began, seek it among those who received it from God Himself."*
>
> - St. Elizabeth Ann Seton

So, What Does and Doesn't Work?

1. Visual aids (whether on a screen or in your hand) are good if they serve a purpose and only if they serve a purpose.
  • They should serve to emphasize an important or *major* point in your talk/presentation.

2. Don't use a prop for the sake of a prop.

3. Do not use a PowerPoint for the sake of using it; be sure you need it. Sometimes PowerPoint can become a crutch and can possibly even stifle the movement of the Holy Spirit.

4. Dress for success. Dress in something that you feel good and look good in. Confidence shows. When you dress for how you want to feel, it's a reflection on the inside, and it shows in our posture and everything else we do.

Manage the Audience

1. Don't ask the group open-ended questions — it invites digression. In doing so, you relinquish control. State a question to "consider" silently, but don't ask it unless it is in context of a large group dialogue.

2. Pay attention to the teen's body language, it will tell you more than anything else about whether or not your message is being received.

3. Remember, it's a dialogue, not a monologue. That doesn't mean inviting the audience to talk, it means recognizing in their responses (silence, laughter, attention or lack of, etc.) if the message is getting through or not.
   • If you're not funny, don't try to be funny. Forced humor is not funny; it is painful and turns off the listeners very quickly. You don't need to be funny as badly as you need to be authentically yourself.

4. Leave them with something practical — a challenge, a commissioning, or something they can immediately implement into their daily faith walk. Abstract is not memorable, practical is what changes lives.

Evaluation

Listen back to your talks and break them apart. Don't be afraid to self-evaluate. And most importantly, don't get down on yourself.

Evaluate

> 1. Take time at the end of the Life/Edge Night to affirm and evaluate the entire night.
>
> 2. Share with one another honestly on how things could be improved and what stood out to you as a strength in the night, including (but not limited to) the presentation.
>
> 3. Accept any feedback, good and bad, as an opportunity to grow and get better. The goal is to reach teens and direct them to Christ, not to glorify ourselves. Always strive for this to be an opportunity to acknowledge what needs to change in order to lead teens closer to Christ.

Be Prepared for Spiritual Attack

After every Proclaim, you may face a certain level of spiritual attack:
• You will recall all that you forgot to mention, all you didn't say or do.
• You will beat yourself up for this and will feel defeated from time to time.
• You will seek out affirmation or validation from other leaders to be sure you did a good job. It's

human, yes, but it's not necessary. Seek your identity and affirmation from God, not man. This is normal but not of God!

Seek Your Core Team for Honest Feedback
(as mentioned above)

- Be careful not to compare yourself to other speakers or Core Members: God called *you* to give this talk for a reason.
- Simply trust that the Lord will and has used you for His glory.

Offer up and Surrender All to the Lord

- If you have prayed through the talk, prepared well, and did your best, God cannot ask for anything more.
- If you failed to give it your all, learn from this mistake and try harder next time.

> "Hold firmly that our faith is identical with that of the ancients. Deny this, and you dissolve the unity of the Church."
>
> - St. Thomas Aquinas

OFFERING A TESTIMONY

Offering a testimony (or witness) is less about sharing what the Church teaches, as it is more about what God has revealed to you through life experience. Now, obviously, this doesn't mean your personal "opinion" on anything doctrinal — far from it. This is a moment to verbalize how God has and is moving in your life. Many times a witness will focus on what God did in your life years ago, a time when He brought you out of darkness into His glorious light... and that's great, but a testimony is far more than that. Authentic conversion happens not once but *daily*. God is constantly crashing into our existence to reveal to us His mercy, providence, and love. Pay attention, in your prayer, to how and where God is moving in your life, and develop not solely your "conversion" testimony, but also, work toward articulating your daily walk with the Lord through life's most common storms, large and small.

> "Our knowledge of Jesus is in need above all of a living experience: Another person's testimony is certainly important, as in general the whole of our Christian life begins with the proclamation that comes to us from one or several witnesses. But we ourselves must be personally involved in an intimate and profound relationship with Jesus."
>
> - *Pope Benedict XVI, October 4, 2006 Rome*

Preparation

What is a Testimony?

1. A testimony is a sharing about what God has done in your life. To be clear, testimonies do not have to be long, do not have to involve your "first" or initial conversion, and do not have to be a spiritual "rags to riches" story. In all honesty, the most effective testimonies are not set far in the past as a one-time conversion, but rather, what God is presently doing in your life in small or large ways.

2. Your testimony might focus on a way God called you to trust and what happened when you did. Your witness might focus less on the sin you struggled with than the freedom and joy you've experienced since overcoming that sin through God's grace and the Sacraments. Your testimony might share your former doubts, yes, but should focus more on practical steps you used to grow in trust.

3. Your testimony's *focus should not be on you* but, rather, what the Holy Spirit has done or is doing *in you* (Galations 2:20).

Execution

The next question is, "How do I share my testimony," and how do I "condense" it into something presentable, engaging, and palatable for teens? Giving a solid testimony takes as much, if not more, work than offering a solid teaching.

1. A testimony needs to be concise, tight, and impactful while maintaining its authenticity, tone, and flow.

- You should create a "short form" (two-to-three minutes) and "long form" (seven-to-ten minutes) in which you keep the main details consistent, but lengthen or shorten given the situation and attention span of those to whom you're speaking.

2. Your testimony should be constructed in a way that can be given at any time, in a formal or informal setting. You never know when God is going to call upon you to share it. It is one of the greatest gifts God has given you to share.

3. You can develop far more than one testimony over time, too, and you should once you have experience giving your primary one.

The "Do-Not's" of Giving Your Testimony

1. Do not share in great detail about just how "sinful" and decadent a life you led. You can make the point without overemphasizing details. Many people unwittingly almost "empower" teens to sin in this way — some teens can walk away thinking, "well, he was this way when he was in college and look how holy he is now." That result is obviously the antithesis of our goal.

2. Do not share about a struggle you are still struggling with — that is off limits. Likewise, do not share about a struggle that you are having that might, in any way, jeopardize any other people in the room (i.e. talking about a breakup with someone who might be known to many others present).

3. Do not confuse a testimony with your autobiography. Less is more. The entire background of your life story is not necessary to share your testimony. Have a watch, and watch your time.

4. Do not confuse a testimony with a self-help seminar or counseling session. While testimonies can sometimes elicit emotions, it is not a rule. A testimony can be funny, serious, emotional, etc., but should always be authentic. You're not "presenting" your testimony, you're sharing it — any passion or tone should flow from the authentic posture of your heart, not from a desire to get an emotional response from others.

The "Do's" of Giving Your Testimony

- Be authentic.
- Be transparent.
- Be yourself.
- Be prepared.
- Be conscious of time.
- Be conscious of how it fits into the larger night/session.
- Be immersed in prayer before, during, and after.

Evaluation

It's supremely difficult to evaluate a testimony in an unbiased way. Be cautious not to "judge" it by the fruit it (immediately) bears. Remember, a testimony is given not only to glorify God, but also, to open the eyes of another to how God is and has been moving *in their lives* as they listen to an account of how He has moved in yours.

If someone offers you an affirmation or words of praise, graciously thank them and offer all glory to God not only for His faithfulness to you, but for the fact that He has revealed these movements to you through the active power of His Holy Spirit. Use

> "Modern man listens more willingly to witnesses than to teachers, and if he does listen to teachers, it is because they are witnesses."
>
> - Pope Paul VI

that moment as a reminder of God's love and enduring presence in your own life, and thank Him for the humble privilege of using you in a small way to further His Kingdom on earth.

PREACHING OR LEADING PRAYER

"And they went forth and preached everywhere, while the Lord worked with them and confirmed the message by the signs that attended it" (Mark 16:20).

Preaching is probably the most unique "presentation" style you may be asked to employ with young souls. Even the most gifted homilists can struggle with preaching to modern teens.

> *"The truest style of oratory, and the most difficult to achieve, is that which seems simple and easy, and leaves the listener with the impression that he could have done just as well himself. The efficacy of preaching lies in plain and natural instruction about the duties of everyman."*
>
> - St. Dominic Barberi

To be clear, preaching is not the same as teaching and should not be approached the same way. If you are preaching at an XLT or night of praise, for instance, our preparation should reflect a difference given the uniqueness of the event, and if Adoration follows, the powerful solemnness that such prayer necessitates. When preaching, you are not merely sharing the teachings of Christ or solely how He has moved in your life, but you are preparing young hearts to have an intimate encounter with the God of the universe.

So what is the "secret" to soul-inspiring preaching? What should we do differently in the preparation process to ensure that we are setting those listening up for a powerful encounter of the living God?

Preparation

If you are a priest or deacon preaching a homily, a topic is pretty clearly laid out in the cycle of readings, but what about when the topic is your choice? How do you decide what to preach about for an "XLT-type" night of praise or worship?

Do you just "go with what God is putting on your heart"? Then you must ask yourself, "How do I know if God is giving this to me, personally, or to be shared publicly? How do I discern the difference? What steps do I take?" Surely, not *everything* God puts on our hearts is intended for others.

Checks and Balances

1. What "system" do you use to discern what is for others, and what God intended solely for you?

a. Spiritual directors are invaluable in this regard.

b. Substantial time in Adoration helps the process, as well.

c. Journaling can often aid in filtering what God wants shared.

d. Frequently ask yourself if what you are planning to preach is going to bring comfort to the afflicted or affliction to the comfortable (and don't shy away from the latter).

2. What Scriptural, catechetical, or saintly input can you use to "check" yourself, your points, and your topic?

• Cross-reference your intended points with official

Church documents and teachings, frequently – even on topics you know well – to remain consistent and offer the wisdom of Mother Church and not just your own.

3. How do you prepare your energy level and tone in order to meet your audience in a prayerful way?

a. Will you be transitioning out of Adoration of the Blessed Sacrament? A time of worship? Silent time?

i. If the praise will be higher energy and spiritually "raucous" before you begin, be sure to meet that energy level and not start too flat.

ii. If the praise will have gone from loud and high energy to something more peaceful and contemplative before you start, be sensitive not to come out of the gate too overexcited or in too high of a speaking gear.

b. Will you be transitioning into Adoration of the Blessed Sacrament? Prayer teams? Silent time? And is the conclusion of your message designed to seamlessly lead into the different time of prayer?

c. Are you well-prepared enough that *you* could enter into the praise preceding you, or direct the audience into praise following you? If not, it's time to either prepare more or trust the Holy Spirit more... you should *always* be present to the time of prayer before you preach since you are a child of God, first, and a preacher (a distant) second.

> "He must increase, but I must decrease."
>
> (John 3:30)

Execution

Pray Hard

Invite the Spirit to lead you and make you His own instrument from start to finish.
- If you have prayed, trust your instincts when reading the room.
- Don't feel chained by your outline but don't abandon it, either.
- Read the room, and the people within it.
  - Allow your verbal pace, pentameter, and tone to dictate to the listeners which points convict you and which ought to convict them.
  - Don't be afraid of silence.
  - Don't be afraid to challenge.
  - Don't be afraid to show vulnerability.
  - Don't be afraid to pray within the preaching.

Respond but Don't React

If the message doesn't seem to be "hitting" home, switch gears but don't necessarily abandon ship.
- Sometimes the eyes of the soul need time to dilate when the Light of Christ begins crashing in. Sometimes stillness or silence in the audience is actually a good sign that they are contemplating or being challenged. Be sure to gauge the faces of the whole not just the few.

Don't Be Afraid to End Early

This is a good rule of thumb for speaking, in general. If you've made your point, sit down; it is especially true of preaching.
- Don't beleaguer your points or your audience.
- Sometimes people don't need to hear any more.

- Less can, indeed, be more. Sometimes you can accomplish more in ten minutes than 25.

Remember *Who* this Is About

Even if you have great things planned to say, the point of preaching is to lead people to an encounter with Christ, not yourself.

> *"And they went forth and preached everywhere, while the Lord worked with them, and confirmed the message by the signs that attended it."*
>
> *(Mark 16:20)*

If you are leading into more prayer time – especially Adoration of the Blessed Sacrament – leave them with a question or two to ponder in the Lord's presence. Something to help them draw their attention back to Him if it wanders or fades.
- You might need, as well, to factor in a couple minutes of pastoral direction regarding proper posture, etc., upon exposition.

Evaluation

It's difficult to evaluate preaching on content since, if we are listening to the Spirit, He could inspire something completely beyond or in lieu of what we had "planned." That being said, ask yourself the following questions:

1. Did I get out of the Spirit's way and allow the Lord to work through me?
   - St. Bernard used the analogy that when the Holy Spirit works through us we are not so much a hose for the Spirit to run through but a fountain by which the Holy Spirit fills us and then overflows upon all in our vicinity.

2. Did *you feel* filled by the Spirit while preaching? Yes or no? Why or why not?
- Did the hearts in the room enter into the following prayer time or activity seamlessly?
- Was there a perceived depth to the prayer in the room — silence or involvement or both?
- Was it a peaceful transition to the prayer time, or was there a great deal of distraction and shuffling about?

3. In the conversations that follow the night, ask teens what God spoke to them, revealed to them, or put on their hearts during the prayer time.
- Don't seek affirmation, seek His glory by focusing on what God was doing and not "how you did."

4. If you are able to record it, go back and listen to what you preached and particularly key into lines you say that you feel were directly inspired by the Holy Spirit.
- Record them in a journal and pray with them in silence, ask the Lord to sharpen and refine your hearing to discern His voice even more easily and clearly in the future.

SECTION TWO:
REFINEMENT

Perhaps speaking to teens has become "old hat" or quite familiar. What are some ways that you can continue to refine the craft? How can you get even better, avoid becoming predictable in your presentations, and take your talks from regularly good to consistently great?

GOING FROM GOOD TO GREAT

Scale Your Talk(s)

The more you practice "scaling" your presentations, the more ways you are giving the Lord to utilize you in different settings should He call upon you to share His truth(s).

1. Do you know your content well enough to cut it in half or expand it by five minutes if necessary?

2. Do you know "where" in the talk you'd add or subtract?

    a. Plan a 15-minute talk as your skeleton.

b. Next, reduce it to five minutes, knowing which elements you could easily cut without sacrificing the point.

c. Then inflate the 15-minute talk to 30 minutes and see if you can keep it cohesive in tone and energy without digression or losing your train of thought.

Storytelling is an Art Form

1. Listen to good storytellers before you tell a story.

    a. Comedians are great at this. They have refined their stories over repeated tellings to live audiences to maximize humor and minimize superfluous details.

    b. TED talks also offer great examples of short storytelling that pack a good deal of information into a concise outline and flow.

    c. Search out talks on YouTube or from apostolates like Lighthouse Catholic Media from some of the best Catholic speakers to youth (several are interviewed in this book) and pay attention to the way they tell stories to teens in a live setting.

2. This is an area you can never grow too much in. Great storytellers can always improve.

    a. Record yourself telling a story you've told frequently.

> *i.* Next, listen to it and identify areas that need less detail and any that might require more detail to really set the tone.
>
> *ii.* Identify places where you could inject either more humor or more depth.

> *b.* Now pay attention to your descriptors. What adjectives and verbs do you use to paint the picture?
>
> *i.* Do you use passive or active verbs? (Hint: avoid passive verbs.)
>
> *ii.* Do you use the same adjectives repeatedly?

> *c.* Practice your pace and pentameter during the story, varying each where necessary.
>
> *i.* Do you provide enough pauses for people to catch their breath after laughing?
>
> *ii.* Do you provide a quick break for deeper truths or dramatic moments to sink in?

Pay Attention to the Little Things.

If you know your talk well enough, it's going to go well enough. But, just in case it's always good to have what I call a crosier (like a Bishop's crosier).

Say you start strong, and even if you have done everything right and according to plan, the talk begins to derail for some reason. Your "crosier" is a verse, a prayer, a story. This is the rip chord to my parachute, this is knowing where I'll go if a talk begins to tank.

What is Your Crosier?

Ask yourself, what is the one fail-safe that I can use to get back on track if I lose my audience?

    a. Is it a saint story that illuminates a point?

    b. A scripture verse that sheds light on the theme?

    c. A personal anecdote that pertains to the topic?

THINGS TO BE AWARE OF, AVOID, OR REMEMBER

We must remember that a great talk is far more than information given or well-received. A great talk is about a connection with the listener's heart as much as their head; great talks penetrate the soul.

I often find that in sharing my failures – my incredibly numerous, amazingly painful, and eternally humbling failures – that people are actually helped. Here are some things to watch out for (experienced by yours truly) when presenting:

- Don't allow keynotes to become a crutch. Allow an image to show beauty. Teens are sharing beauty, or the lack of it, on Instagram. We have the opportunity in an Instagram culture to connect the secular to the sacred. We have the opportunity to say, "what do you see when you look at that?" and respond "I see God, and the creator of creation." Our visuals should reinforce that point.

- We should spend more time practicing, with authenticity and rawness.

- When we haven't prepared for how, or what part of the Scriptures we might read, it's not going to come off as real to the teens that receive the Word we proclaim.

- Each Beatitude is less than 140 characters, the entire Sermon on the Mount is ten minutes long... humanity is conditioned in this way. We aren't normally conditioned to listen for 45 minutes or longer. We shouldn't be shocked when kids can only sit for so long.

• Jesus chose to teach through humor, relationship, visuals, etc. — constantly linking creation to the creator. He used visual aids, and we can as well, but we have to be thoughtful and intentional about the visual aids we choose.

• You are speaking on behalf of the Roman Catholic Church. Your opinion doesn't matter. You have been called by God, empowered and charged to proclaim the truth of Christ and His Church. Your personal opinion has no bearing and no relevance in this setting. The Church has truth, and you lean on the truth. If you cannot answer a question — remember the Church can answer, and you have the resources to find the answer. Do not fear the tough topics. Teens will leave if you give them vanilla. You have to give them the rich and bold flavor of the Truth.

• If you're not funny, don't try to be. If God did not give you that gift, He has given you another gift. Be yourself.

• Prepare a talk, but don't obsess about it.

• Don't assume that your audience wants to know every detail about your life.

• Don't talk about something you're still healing from. You do not have proper perspective yet.

TEN "DO'S" AND "DON'TS" WHEN SPEAKING TO TEENS

What makes a "great" talk? Think about all the talks you have ever heard. What spoke to you? What engaged you? Which talks moved you so powerfully that it literally changed your life?

When you think about questions like these and about all the talks you have heard, the things most of us remember are the ones that connected with us personally. The personal stories, the way a speaker was able to make a "picture" out of what he or she was saying, and humor — many of the funny stories we have heard at camps or retreats as a teenager we still remember today.

When we attempt to put together a resource on what makes a "great talk," it is necessary to include the basic components. Section Three, of this resource is filled with great talk outlines by some of the best speakers in Catholic Youth Ministry. But let's look first at the basic "framework" of a good talk.

Five Key Elements that Help Talks "Succeed"

1. Humor

Some of the greatest talks you remember are the ones that kept you laughing, and laughing, and then all of a sudden – bam – they hit you square in the face with their point! The humor catches you off guard and the blow is dramatic — and life-changing in some cases. The humor is not humor for humor's sake. The laughter drops defenses and shatters walls around head and heart. In the boxing match that is catechesis, the laughter is the jab that sets up the listener for the uppercut of truth. For teenagers, it's tough to give a "great" or memorable talk without at least *some* humor. Get 'em laughing and you got 'em. Bore 'em, and you might as well quit before you start.

All that being said, some presenters are naturally humorous and others, clearly, are not.

If you are not naturally funny, that's okay. See if there is some way to incorporate a little humor. An amusing video clip or image can work well, as can a quick anecdote or random story that may not further the topic but might accentuate a shared or typical human emotion (i.e. nervousness, awkwardness, etc.). The point being, don't try to be someone you are not and don't attempt to do stand-up comedy, but realize that humor with any crowd – especially teens – is a very useful tool if used correctly.

2. Stories

God, Himself, demonstrated time and again in the Gospels that the story was His preferred method of evangelization and catechesis. There's a reason the Son of God employed this teaching method and I'd submit we ought to learn from His example. Nothing captures listeners better than stories: personal examples that bring the message to life and give it flesh. There obviously is a need for healthy boundaries with this — youth ministers and Core Members need to have sensitivity about how much detail they share about their personal struggles. There is not a need to share all the gory details of past sins or struggles. However, for a talk to be "good," it is critical to connect with your audience. And there is no better way to do that then to have them identify personally with you, or by capturing their imagination with a great story.

3. Grabbing their Attention Early

Every talk has a starting point — and it's your only chance to make sure that your audience is going to listen to the rest of what you have to say. Open well, and capture them, and you have a chance of taking them the distance. On the other hand, open poorly, and you'll be lucky to recover. A good speaker will usually spend the most time rehearsing their opening and closing (which we'll cover next). It needs to be crisp and engaging — the idea is to create a "door" for the audience to walk through into the rest of the talk.

4. Less is More

When planning a talk, make sure you set a realistic goal for how much information you can communicate. It all depends on the group you are speaking to. If you have a group of leadership teens, you can go longer and get across more material. If you're talking to "un-churched" or younger teens, you need to limit your content significantly. And whichever teen demographic you have, your content needs to be arranged in a clear, easy-to-follow way. You want to be careful not to lose your listeners in the navigation of the talk. Create a pathway that everyone can follow — with clear signposts. It's good to have three to five points maximum. Make your points clear, re-articulating them a couple times throughout the talk, and highlight them again in your closing.

5. So, now what?

Finally, every good talk needs to answer the question, "so, now what?" before you finish, especially for teens. Make the message relevant to their lives, and give them something concrete — what does this content mean in relation to the way they live their life? At times, an opportunity for a personal response or a commitment of some type may even be appropriate. Give them something practical to implement in their life that night or that week.

Five Places Where Talks "Fail"

1. Problem: No Bearings — we misjudge where the teens are spiritually.

Many times we lose teens before we ever have them. We throw out words they don't know the meaning of and phrasing they couldn't care less about. No matter how well versed your group is catechetically, it helps to consider them as TSL students (Theology as a Second Language).

Now, this obviously doesn't mean talk down to them, nor does it mean treat them like idiots. It means recognizing that even though some might know the definition of a word, it doesn't mean they comprehend the essence of it. You might have students who can define dogma and doctrine but have yet to surrender to the beauty of the Church's authority. You might have teens who know the Church's teaching on the sacraments and the Eucharist but have no concept of what grace is, means, or does. I once experienced a youth minister stand in front of his audience and read straight out of the Catechism, paragraphs at a time, because they enraptured his own soul so intensely... by the second line, I was already wondering if this exercise could be used to cure clinical insomniacs.

Solution: Really take advantage of that time prior to and following youth group activities as well as other teen gatherings to get to know teens on a more relational level, when they're not looking for the million-dollar answer during small groups. The better you know them on a relational level, the more aware you'll be of their vocabulary and the need to translate "Church speak."

2. Problem: Poor Preparation
— our talk preparation supercedes our prayer.

Look at the percentage of time you spend preparing your talking points for a teaching, or rehearsing the content. Now, compare that to the time you spent, in preparation, praying about all aspects of your talk and not just about the delivery.

   • Have you prayed for the teens that will be there, for the soil of their hearts to be tilled? Have you prayed for the other Core Members on the night?
   • Have you prayed for the parents of the teens who will be waiting for them at home, that their hearts might reaffirm the truths of the Church that you are sharing?

If our time praying does not eclipse our time preparing and memorizing notes, we're disordered. And, if we're not praying at all, then we are definitely not dialed into the Holy Spirit. So, when things inevitably go wrong or teens disengage mid-talk, we won't be equipped to discern what to do or how to adjust on the fly.

It's not just about sharing the word of God (Scripture) but the Living Word of God: Jesus Christ. If we're not intimately connected to Him in prayer, it's probably not Him we're sharing but us.

Solution: Spend more time in prayer than you do creating outlines or practicing. Consider a 2/1 ratio — pray twice as much as you prep.

3. Problem: Poor Transitions — we're unaware of the setup and handoff.

The Setup: Do you know what is happening immediately prior to your talk? I don't mean what is scheduled to happen (on the catechetical outline for the night), but how the room is responding to what is happening?

- Is there a skit and is it flopping?
- Was there a video and were the teens watching or talking through it?
- Has there been any prayer?
- Is the tone and mood of the room "up" or "down" prior to your talk, and how will that affect your tone when you begin?

The Handoff: How about what comes after your talk?

- Will there be small groups, a large group discussion, or personal prayer time?
- How does your talk set up what comes next?
  ◦ Are you preparing their hearts for deep discussion or reflection?
  ◦ Is the desired mood and tone of the room to be "up" or "down" when you finish and are you prepared to get them there?

This is such a crucial point when preparing a talk, and often times, the one that is most overlooked. It's easy to get so consumed with "what I have to say" that we forget the talk is one piece – one minor piece – to the overall puzzle that is catechesis.

Can you think of anything worse than a talk that doesn't end? The speaker has made their point, sometimes even powerfully, but then for some reason, just keeps talking and talking. They keep circling the runway, seemingly unable to actually land the plane. You know you need to end, but you just can't figure out how. It's one of the reasons why good speakers spend a lot of time figuring out how they want to end. They usually will have more than one ending rehearsed so they can end from different points in the talk. There are many times that you realize that the talk is over before you are — in those times, forget what ever else you have planned, and LAND THE PLANE!

Solution: Know your content well enough to be anxiety-free as the night begins. Be out greeting the teens. Participate in the gathering activities, games, music, and opening prayer. Know what happens after your talk, and be humble enough to "hit a single" if that is what the night necessitates. Not every talk needs to be a home run.

4. Problem: We're too Rigid — our message isn't malleable or "scaleable."

Is your talk a speech? If so, it's time to change perspective. Often times, people prepare a talk like they would a speech. It contains everything in a specific order. While there's nothing wrong with that, it can present difficulties on occasion, especially in a ministry setting.

What if the night is running long because a Gather activity took forever to get going or get cleaned up? You now only have five minutes for a ten-minute speech (er, I mean, talk) that you prepared.

- Will you know where to cut it?
- Is it "scalable" — meaning can you scale it down or beef it up, as needed?
- What about if two teens are distracting others (and you) in the midst of your talk, and you lose your place?

If it's a speech, it can be tricky to get back on track. What if the mood of the room is different than you anticipated (as we spoke about in number three), can you adjust to that on the fly without jumping from point to point or losing your emphasis?

Solution: Rather than preparing your entire talk as a speech, work off of key words and phrases (as I discussed earlier in this resource). Write those key words and phrases on a large index card so if, God forbid, you lose your place, seeing that one word or phrase will trigger your next point. If you have to write out a speech, be sure to be able to outline it or boil it down to smaller points. Know those points well enough to eliminate points, if needed, without running your train of thought off the rails.

5. Problem: Not in a State of Grace — sinners can't lead sinners out of sin.

When was the last time you went to confession? The Sacrament of Reconciliation is the greatest weapon and most untapped source of grace for any presenter. Do we go forward to speak and teach in God's name without being in a state of grace? That's like walking into the operating room to perform surgery while blindfolded, with earplugs in, and oven mitts on. We need to free ourselves from every sin weighing us down. We need to be grace-filled and free to boldly proclaim God's truth without our humanity and pride getting in the way.

People trapped in sin cannot lead others trapped in sin out of sin.

Solution: If needed, get to the parish on Saturday (or early on Sunday) and reconcile with Christ in the Sacrament. It will make all the difference in this world and the next.

If we all follow these five reminders, our next talk will be perfect, right? No, but it will go a lot further in both building the Kingdom and achieving our own sanctity. I hope you go easier on yourself than I do on myself. I pray that God goes easier on all of us than we deserve. Approach every opportunity to speak as an awe-inspiring gift from God, that He would entrust such an incredible charge – proclaiming His good news – to people like us! That humility will take the talk to places we never could.

SECTION THREE:
BEHIND THE SCENES

INTERVIEWS WITH SEVERAL EFFECTIVE CATHOLIC YOUTH SPEAKERS

Jackie (Francois) Angel
Mary Bielski
Leah Darrow
Jason Evert
Matt Fradd
Bob Rice
Chris Stefanick
Joel Stepanek

JACKIE (FRANCOIS) ANGEL

What are some of the steps, beyond prayer, that you regularly employ when preparing a talk for teenagers?

Beyond prayer, I normally make a short outline of three bullet points that I want to get across in the talk. Under each bullet point, I'll try to reference a verse from Scripture and include an example or story. Sometimes under a bullet point, I'll use a video clip or pop song to demonstrate the point. I always try to start out a talk with humor. Whether it's making fun of myself, telling a funny story that happened, or sharing some relevant pop culture, humor always draws people in and makes them feel more at ease. Some teens will come to a talk with a very skeptical or defensive demeanor, but when you use humor, it breaks down the walls they might have and opens up their hearts to listen to the message.

What are three or four things you tell youth leaders (or try to model for them) to remain conscious of when executing a talk for teens?

1. <u>Be authentic</u>. You don't have to be crazy and outgoing to be a good speaker, but you should be passionate about the subject. Whether you have more of a preacher

or a teacher style of speaking, being authentic means living out what you are saying. If you are speaking on chastity, yet you yourself are deep into pornography or sleeping with another Core Member, teens can easily sniff out the hypocrisy. In the encyclical, *Evangelii Nuntiandi,* Pope Paul VI said that the world will more willingly listen to witnesses than teachers, but if they do listen to teachers it is because they are first witnesses.

2. Don't read from a script. Let your talk flow naturally and tell stories from your life. You can hit teens over the head with catechetical stuff, but when you share how that same "stuff" has affected your life, teens listen because stories are powerful. It says in Revelation 12:11 that the devil will be defeated by the blood of the lamb and the word of their testimony. Your testimony and how God has worked in your life is powerful and can really help teens to see God in day-to-day life and their own lives.

3. Humor and joy are great things. A lot of times teens won't remember a word you said, but they'll remember your presence, especially your joy. Most teens think that being Catholic is boring, so when they see a joyful witness who can laugh at him or herself (or make them laugh), it is a refreshing thing.

How do you evaluate a talk once you've given it? What criteria do you use in deciding if it was as effective as possible or to help you improve in the future?

One thing you can use to evaluate is the teens' body language. Are they yawning, rolling their eyes, or sleeping? Normally a few kids out of a hundred will do this, but if the majority are looking bored, then you might realize you are not connecting with them. If teens are leaning forward, laughing, smiling, listening intently, crying, cheering, or giving you a standing ovation, then I would say you may have won them over. Seriously, though, watching body language is very important for a speaker to know how to shift the talk. For me, I can also tell if my talk was really choppy or if it flowed really well, and use that as an indicator. Sometimes, the time goes by very fast and I can't even remember a whole lot of what I said, which probably means the Holy Spirit did most of the work!

What has your vast experience speaking to teens taught you over the years? What bit of wisdom would you want to share with youth ministers and Core Members?

Teens won't remember your talk; they will remember your presence. I know this doesn't help when you're trying to formulate a good talk, but teens will remember your passion, your joy, your faith, and your witness. Don't sweat it if you haven't memorized the whole Bible. Teens notice if you are living it.

How do you pray before, during, and after a talk? What do you do to ensure it's God on whom you are leaning, and not yourself?

Before the talk, the Eucharist at Daily Mass is my source of strength and energy, and Mary is the one who I always ask to intercede for me; that the Holy Spirit might speak through me. If I get to go to Adoration before my talk, that's an extra bonus! During the talk (especially if there's a break to watch a video clip, etc.), I'll keep praying, "Come, Holy Spirit!" After the talk, I'll thank God profusely for being so generous with His Spirit and often I'll pray a rosary for the teens to whom I just spoke. I always kick myself when I don't pray well before or after my talk, because I know that I'm relying on my own strength and not God's.

Biography
Jackie is a full-time traveling speaker, singer/songwriter, and worship leader from Orange County, CA. In 2006, she became an artist with OCP/SpiritandSong.com with whom she has released two albums. She has been involved in youth ministry since she graduated high school, and she now travels the globe speaking to young people about God's love and leading worship for various events and ministries. She is friends with people who are passionate about God, food, and coffee. and perhaps saints, spiritual books, volleyball, quoting stupid things, the beach, accents, and bowling. Check out iTunes or SpiritandSong.com to get Jackie's albums "Your Kingdom is Glorious" and "Divine Comedy."

Find Jackie on Social Media:
Twitter.com/JackieFrancois
Instagram.com/jackiefrancois
Facebook.com/ JackieFrancoisMusic

MARY BIELSKI

What are some of the steps, beyond prayer, that you regularly employ when preparing a talk for teenagers?

Stage 1
Things to Consider Before Writing Your Talk:

- Know your audience
- Know your goal/ purpose
- Know the type of talk you are giving ("How to" vs. "Why" talks)
- Know the surrounding details (time, tone, and placing in the event flow) etc.

Stage 2
Brainstorm, Research, and Illustration:

Once you have your *central goal of the talk*, you can start building the supporting points. You will need to brainstorm and research to develop your talking points.

Brainstorm: Ask important questions before developing talking points.
  ◦ Why is this topic important or relevant to teens?

- What are some messages (good and bad) from culture, parents, and peers being told to the audience?
- What is the central truth about Christ and the Church?
- What are the three or four most vital points to this truth that every teen should know?
- Brainstorm personal stories relevant to this topic.
- Why is this topic meaningful to my life? How did I come to know the truth of this teaching? Where have I struggled to believe this, why?
- Is there a story of a family member, friend or youth that is connected to this story?
- What is the one thing I want to leave the audience with to encourage them?

Research: Research your topic using a variety of resources and look for ideas and other illustrations and stories that can help.
- Church teaching: Bible, biblical commentaries, catechism, and books
- Cultural messages: Teen Culture (YouTube, eNews, Twitter feeds, Magazines, Commercials, Billboard music, TMX)
- External stories: Blogs, other preachers, sermons on line, podcasts, etc.

Illustration: *Talks come alive through stories and illustrations.* An illustration is an image, video, or story that gives an example to what you are talking about. Christ taught through parables. He used examples (seeds, farming, lending, etc.) of things that were common to the people at the time to help them understand. We must do the same. Having good, relevant, illustrations are key to an effective and powerful talk!

Other Resources that may help you:

- Biblical Commentaries: Book of Matthew (Edward Sri); Book of Luke (Timothy Johnson); Book of Mark (Mary Healy); Book of John (Craig Keener)
- Scott Hahn's Catholic Dictionary
- Authors I would suggest: Scott Hahn and Brant Pitre (easy to follow on topic of faith)
- Podcasts and sermons: Fr. Barron, Fr. Mike Schmidt's, Fr. Mark Toups, and Dr. Tom Neil

Stage 3
Develop your Points:

Once you have brainstormed and researched, you should have a main topic and two-to-four points that you want to use to support it. Then, spend time fleshing out each of the points. Many times we use words that don't mean anything to teens or may have a different meaning because of culture (like: salvation, grace, transformation, love, justification, etc.) *You need to connect the dots for the teens.* Don't assume they understand what you are talking about.

Here are three questions I use to do that well.

1. What is the teaching or point?

    a. For Example: The Church is a Body of Christ (*CCC* 787-795)

2. What does that mean?

    a. For Example: Just like a body has a nervous, skeletal, and skin, each part of the community is working differently to serve the whole... (describe what this means).

3. What does that look like? (Provide Illustration: story, image, video etc.)

    a. For Example:

        i. When my sister died, I saw the way the community came together like a body.

        ii. When I was young. I didn't get St. Paul's description, until I saw a, b, c...

        iii. I read this article that explained how the church responded to Hurricane Katrina, listen to what it said. Here you can see how the members came together... (etc.)

Note: Keep in mind, you always are trying to highlight why this point is important, so draw stories that the audience can identify with and point it back to them. Many talks I see have all the head (what is it) but miss the story or illustration. Other talks have great stories, but miss the theology. *We need to capture both: the head and the heart.*

Stage 4
Put it within a Structure:

    I. Introduction — draw in the crowd with a story.

    II. Main Thesis — make clear the talk purpose. Where you are going and why it's important?

    III. 3-4 Supporting points
        a. For each: what is it, what does that mean, what does that look like (illustration/story)?

    IV. Conclusion — call to action

Stage 5
Practice, Rework, and Evaluate:

Each presenter has a different style of writing and presenting talks. Some write them word for word while others outline the talks with bullet points. Do whatever works for you, but I would suggest that you do not read your talk word for word. It is more natural if you are comfortable enough to talk through without just reading it. You can use notes if that is helpful. For me, I used to memorize my talks ten years ago. Now I know my outlines and let the Spirit do the rest. But do what works for you; practice and prepare so you feel confident when you come on stage.

Presenting is a craft as well. Knowing when to speed up your pace, slow down, or pause will help draw your audience in. Tempo, flow, and transitions in the talk are important to help emphasize the content. This comes with watching other presenters and learning as well as trial and error.

What are three or four things you tell youth leaders (or try to model for them) to remain conscious of when executing a talk for teens?

1. <u>Be Relevant</u>
If the talk does not answer the question: "so what?" it doesn't do it's job. Connect your content to your audience, their life, their struggle, and their culture. This is the biggest issue I see with presenters. They present the content, but do not connect the dots to the lives of the listeners. Christ is a God that wants to speak to the teen's reality of today. The talk should always seek to show how this specific topic has significance in the teen's life and faith. Otherwise it is meaningless.

2. Be Clear

I see many talks that have great stories and funny commentary, but leave you not unsure what the main point was. Make sure you come with your central goal and purpose in mind. Be clear about what the central purpose is. Everything within your talk should point back to that main point.

3. Be Authentic

Vulnerability moves the heart. I will follow any leader who is on their knees. The more we can expose the places of our authentic journey (messy and imperfect) the more we can encourage our teens to be truthful as well. We don't serve the teens by giving them the false understanding that once they follow Jesus life gets easy. Be authentic and let them look into the life of a true disciple. Vulnerability is courageous!

4. Be You

For those who feel unprepared or ill equipped to speak, welcome to the club. We have all heard it said, "God does not call the equipped he equips the called." This gives me comfort. And even as a national speaker, there are many times that I feel unworthy or insecure before getting on stage. There is often a temptation to compare our gifts to others or be critical. But I can't be any other speaker. I have to be me, unique and unrepeatable. Remember that you have a message. Don't try to be someone else when you present. If you are not funny naturally, don't try to be. *Be you!* Your story and witness can make a difference.

How do you evaluate a talk once you've given it? What criteria do you use in deciding if it was as effective as possible or to help you improve in the future?

Sometimes you can get a sense through the reaction of the crowd on how your talk is being received. But I would caution you to make that your primary barometer. Teens often respond more to humor. And if that is not your gift then you can think you flopped. Honestly, sometimes I just don't know how it was received. However, I do know when I am speaking "in the Spirit" and when I am in myself. It feels differently. As much as the Spirit has taught me that over the years, I can't teach that.

On a practical level, I generally need a trusted adult or youth minister who will give me true and specific feedback. I once asked a friend and she said, "it was good, but you went too fast." This is helpful feedback. We need to help each other.

Also, if there are areas you are working on, tell someone so they can help you. I call my sister often to throw out ideas and see what she thinks. I call youth ministers to pick their brains and ask them thoughts and feedback. I try to form a team of people who can help me get better.

I also am self-evaluating constantly. If you can record yourself, that is the most effective means to see where you can grow.

What has your vast experience speaking to teens taught you over the years? What bit of wisdom would you want to share with youth ministers and Core Members?

For many years, I always felt horrible after I gave a talk. The spiritual attack would be epic. Speaking is not always easy. You expose your heart and open yourself up to others criticism. I was the most critical of myself after I spoke. I constantly would nit-pick everything that didn't go well, or what I should have done differently. The biggest advice I have for you is to remember it is not your job to change the hearts of your audience. It is God's. You have no idea what is happening in the hearts and minds of your audience.

This changed for me, when my spiritual director called me out after a particularly frustrating talk. She said, "Mary, when do you get to judge what is good fruit and what is not? Leave that to God." She was right. God doesn't call us to be successful, but faithful. So now, I put the pressure on God, and get my pride out of the way. Learn to laugh at yourself. Learn to love yourself, even in your imperfections. It will make presenting more fun because it isn't about you. It is about your audience, and about the Lord and His goodness.

Trust that God can use your mess.

How do you pray before, during, and after a talk? What do you do to ensure it's God on whom you are leaning, and not yourself?

This takes time and practice to get out of God's way. I have had to learn this by trial and walking daily with God. I pray and fast prior to speaking for the audience. I pray for a humble heart and that God would use me. I also pray daily and vigorously for the spiritual gifts, specifically for prophecy. I pray to be prophetic in the times we are living. And then I trust.

It is a secret mystery how God uses us. And so it only comes with growing with intimacy in prayer that we learn to trust and walk in Him and not ourselves. I know I can't teach you this. Stay at His feet and let Him teach you.

Biography

As the founder of ALL4HIM Ministries in 2006, Mary has spoken to over 75,000 teens around the nation at high school and young adult retreats and conferences, including Steubenville Youth Conferences, Life Teen-Inspiration, and parish and diocesan rallies. Using funny stories and engaging analogies, Mary draws her audience to the beauty of our Catholic faith, a deeper love for Christ, the Eucharist, and the call to holiness.

Mary is currently attaining her masters in Theology at Notre Dame Seminary in New Orleans, LA and enjoying the crawfish! For more information about Mary and her ministry go to www.marybielski.com

Find Mary on Social Media:
Twitter.com/marybielski
Instagram.com/marybielski
Facebook.com/marybielskispeaker

LEAH DARROW

What are some of the steps, beyond prayer, that you regularly employ when preparing a talk for teenagers?

I focus on the below three points for every presentation I give. Outside of prayer and grace, these have been indispensable to me as a public speaker on the stage as well as appearances on TV and the radio.

1. Make Your Point.
I once heard a parent ask their teen after my talk if they liked it. The teen said, "I loved it!" The parent responded, "Awesome, what was her message?" The teen thought for a second and said, "I don't know, but her stories were great." Yikes. While I might be a great storyteller, my stories must make a point. Stories are nothing more than illustrations that should highlight a bigger theme or idea. For example, the story of the prodigal son is not about the son's debacle but the main theme Jesus shares with us is the mercy of the Father. Every presentation should have one central point or theme. Typically, the central theme can have anywhere between two to four (three is preferable) illustrations that signal to the central theme. Make sure you know the point you want to make, and make it.

2. Rehearse Aloud & In Front of a Mirror.

This sounds obvious, but I see this happen all the time with speakers. They rehearse... but inside their head. People want to hear what you have to say, so it's a good idea to practice aloud what they will soon hear.

Rehearsing in front of a mirror is a trick my college acting coach taught me. Every actor and comedian I know still does this. It is essential to see what the audience will see. I rehearse in front of a mirror first by sitting down in a chair so that I rely completely on the content. Once I execute the content, I stand up and allow my personal style (hand gestures, smiles, funny faces, etc.) to be added into the talk.

Tip: Make eye contact with yourself during the entire rehearsal, and be on the look out for filler words such as: um, k, right, you know, like, well, anyway, etc. As soon as you hear them, stop and say the line again without the filler word.

3. Land The Plane.

The hardest part for most speakers (including myself) is ending the talk or in other words, "landing the plane." By the end of the presentation you've probably stopped sweating profusely and are finally getting into the groove and feel like you could go another 20 or 30 minutes. *The heroic moment for any speaker is knowing when to stop speaking and exit the stage.* Once you've made your point, shared the stories to illustrate it, and wrapped up your conclusion, give it all to God and land that plane. I simply end with the phrase, "Thank you so much, God love you and God bless."

What are three or four things you tell youth leaders (or try to model for them) to remain conscious of when executing a talk for teens?

When speaking with teens, it's crucial to remember that the audience will have a wide range of brokenness — some have been through hell and back, some are still in the midst of a dysfunctional lifestyle or home life, and others have never suffered a hangnail. Knowing your audience is key to delivering an effective and appropriate message.

Don't be afraid to laugh at yourself. I personally think humor should be a requirement in every talk, someway, somehow. We all have moments of hilarity in our lives, especially when they involve us trying and failing. Sharing these stories not only lifts spirits but also humanizes you to the crowd.

How do you evaluate a talk once you've given it? What criteria do you use in deciding if it was as effective as possible or to help you improve in the future?

Praise should never be the measure of a talk. If we measure our gifts by the applause-o-meter, we are no longer working for God but for ourselves. Venerable Fulton Sheen was asked once how many people he helped convert to Catholicism. His answer? That he has never counted, and is afraid that if he did, he would think he was responsible for them instead of the Holy Spirit.

However, here are the evaluation tools I use:

1. <u>I record my talk.</u> I used to hate hearing my voice on a recording, but after watching myself on reality TV and the syndicated reruns (why God, why!?), the audio files weren't so bad. I try and listen to the talk as soon as possible so that I can fix any problems before I'm in front of another group of people.

2. <u>I ask someone to critique me.</u> Usually, before my presentation begins, I reach out to a priest, sister, or another adult and ask them to offer me constructive criticism afterwards. If you're really on top of it, you can create a short list of questions on a notecard for them to fill out. *Example:* What was the main message of my talk? Did my stories properly illustrate the main message? What was missing in my talk?

3. <u>I go back over my outline.</u> Did I make my main point? Did I successfully support the main point or theme with my illustrations? Was I honest, genuine, and sensitive to the needs of the audience with my content? If I made the point I was trying to make, shared stories to support the main point, then I can, at least content wise, call it a win. The rest of the finesse that goes into a talk takes time, practice, and His grace.

4. <u>I pay attention to the questions asked after my talk.</u> If I'm asked the same question three or more times, it's a red flag that I need to include that bit of information in the talk.

What has your vast experience speaking to teens taught you over the years? What bit of wisdom would you want to share with youth ministers and Core Members?

One of the biggest lessons I've learned is that it's not about me being a "speaker" — it's about one child of God sharing with other children of God that He loves us, forgives us, and desires our friendship and happiness. At a Life Teen conference, I heard Dr. Scott Hahn say something I'll never forget, he said, "God doesn't just want to love other people through you, He wants to love you!" We sometimes forget that God also wants to love us, not just the souls in the audience. He wants to speak to us, listen to us, and ultimately transform our lives — not for the sake of talk material but for our salvation. There is freedom in allowing Him to love us and allowing that love to flow through a presentation.

How do you pray before, during, and after a talk? What do you do to ensure it's God on whom you are leaning, and not yourself?

Before a talk, I pray a Memorare and a prayer to the Holy Spirit. During a talk, I am praying sometimes for individual souls and other times for the continued peace and clarity to share the intended message. After the presentation is over, I thank God for helping me through the talk and for the opportunity to meet and love His children. I ask Him to perfect all that I failed to do in the talk, and then I ask for His grace to be sealed in the audience and in me.

Anything good I have done or can do is because of Jesus and His grace. To remind me of this truth, I will either say aloud or to myself, "All praise be to God" after any gratitude I receive. I am honored to have a front row seat to the workings of the Holy Spirit but make no mistake about it, while I am cooperating with Jesus it is Jesus who transforms hearts.

Biography
Leah Darrow is a wife, mom, author, speaker, fashionista, and Broadway musical enthusiast. She enjoys engaging culture from a Catholic perspective and challenges people to reclaim love and beauty from a society that has distorted both. She hopes to one day swim with orcas or catch the first sighting of bigfoot, whichever comes first.

Find Leah on Social Media:
Twitter.com/leahdarrow

JASON EVERT

What are some of the steps, beyond prayer, that you regularly employ when preparing a talk for teenagers?

1. Record the talk, and as painful as it might be, listen to it. You'll be able to pluck out flaws in your speaking that you would otherwise never hear. Also, don't be afraid to ask people for some constructive feedback, not just praise. If you can video tape the talk, this is even better. You'll likely notice certain gestures and habits that you may want to change.

2. Do plenty of homework, researching the subject that you will be presenting on. As Sirach 33:4 says, "Prepare what to say, and thus you will be heard; bind together your instruction, and make your answer."

3. Make sure you have prepared a part in the talk on "how to live it out," so that your hearers will not become resentful or despairing. They need to see that Christ's grace is sufficient, and that the advice given is practical.

What are three or four things you tell youth leaders (or try to model for them) to remain conscious of when executing a talk for teens?

1. <u>Use "I" more than "you."</u> Some people will speak to teens and say, "You need to do this, and you need to do that." Instead, talk about your own testimony. For example, you could talk about a mistake you made, and say, "I needed to start respecting myself, so I... " Teens who are in a similar situation will be able to draw upon your experiences and apply it to themselves without feeling judged or accused. In fact, they will find common ground with you, and will be more likely to approach you afterwards.

2. <u>Never read your talk to them</u>. The last time someone read to you, you were a child, and they were trying to put you to sleep. Ideally, be well enough prepared that you don't even need notes. Otherwise, the audience will assume that if you can't remember your talk, why should they? It's fine to have a few notes jotted down to glance at, but the sooner you can do it without notes, the better.

3. <u>Praise and affirm teens </u>— they thrive on it, and they rarely hear it.

4. <u>Smile</u>. Joy makes an impression.

5. If you're going to speak on chastity, make sure of one thing: Explain why chastity can only be thought of in association with the virtue of love. It frees us to love and frees us to know if we are being loved. It's not about waiting until marriage to love your boyfriend or girlfriend, but about loving them perfectly today through your sacrifice.

How do you evaluate a talk once you've given it? What criteria do you use in deciding if it was as effective as possible or to help you improve in the future?

Providing the teens with an anonymous evaluation form is ideal because this allows them to be brutally honest. But since this is not always practical or appropriate, ask a few adults to give you some feedback, including a few positives and a few negatives.

Make yourself available afterwards to interact with the teens. If one says that the talk was really good, ask what it specifically was that helped them.

Do not be obsessed with knowing you hit a home run. God alone knows the fruits that will come. All He asks is that you will be faithful. If your talk was extremely successful in winning souls, God would probably withhold the knowledge of this from you, for your own sake.

You might walk away from a talk, thinking you did a fabulous job, and yet the audience might fall back into their bad habits within hours. Likewise, you might think your talk was terrible, and it may have saved countless souls. It's not within our power to know. If we did, we might be tempted to pride or despair. If you want your talks to bear fruit, pray and fast for your audience members, even after giving your talk. After all, the world was not saved by the Sermon on the Mount, but on Calvary.

What has your vast experience speaking to teens taught you over the years? What bit of wisdom would you want to share with youth ministers and Core Members?

I have heard it said that you cannot change someone unless you love them and they know that you love them. Therefore, a teen may benefit more from a loving youth minister who is a terrible preacher than from the most eloquent orator whose heart is not pure. So don't be too worried about your inadequacies. Even Moses had a speech impediment! So long as you love the teens and God, He'll fill in the gaps.

Ask others to intercede for you. I have written letters to more than 100 convents of nuns, asking them to pray for my family, my ministry, and my audience members. When I see miraculous conversions, I know who to thank.

Lastly, when ministering to teens, I often think of the words of St. John Vianney: "What person X needs for his conversion is your holiness."

How do you pray before, during, and after a talk? What do you do to ensure it's God on whom you are leaning, and not yourself?

Make sure you schedule time in Eucharistic Adoration as part of the preparation of your talk. Soak in the grace of a holy hour. Offer a Rosary, and go over your talk with God, and He will often place new inspirations on your heart. Mother Teresa had a little prayer she called the express novena. She knew that this was so powerful that she would pray it, not so much in petition for something, but in thanksgiving for the fact that she knew she was going to receive it. It consisted of praying the Memorare nine times. You may want to pray this before each talk in thanksgiving for the conversions that will take place, and for the gift of apostolic preaching. You could ask for the eloquence of speech of St. Anthony of Padua, and the effectiveness of speech of Samuel, and for gifts even greater than these.

Invoke the intercession of your guardian angel, and the guardian angels of all of the teens in the room. Even if a student is an atheist, he still has a guardian angel, and so it is wise to take advantage of this heavenly host.

Another one of my favorite prayers, that you can pray before giving a talk, is commonly called the fragrance prayer, which was prayed daily by Mother Teresa:

"Dear Jesus, help me to spread your fragrance everywhere I go. Flood my soul with your spirit and life. Penetrate and possess my whole being so utterly that all my life may only be a radiance of yours. Shine through me, and be so in me that every soul I come in contact with may feel your presence in my soul. Let them look up and see no longer me but only you, dear Jesus! Stay with me, and then I shall begin to shine as you shine; so to shine as to be a light to others. The light, O Lord, will be all from you; none of it will be mine; it will be you, shining on others through me. Let me thus praise you in the way you love best, by shining on those around me. Let me preach you without preaching, not by words, but by my example, by the catching force, the sympathetic influence of what I do, the evident fullness of the love my heart bears to you. Amen."

As a way to follow up the talk with prayer, I sometimes have the teens put their names in a prayer book, which I can later take to Adoration. Then, I use their names as the beads of a Rosary.

Anything else you would want to add? Words of encouragement, wisdom, affirmation, etc.?

Don't forget to fast for your teens (and for all our teens)! To simply pray for them without fasting is like boxing with one arm tied behind your back. But, do not stop with fasting from food: <u>Fast from words</u>. As St. Faustina says, "A talkative soul is empty inside." *Fast from noise*. For starters, take a month off from listening to the radio in the car. This includes even Christian music. As St. John Paul the Great said, "Above all, create silence in your interior. Let that ardent desire to see God arise from the depth of your hearts, a desire that at times is suffocated by the noise of the world and the seduction of pleasures." Through creating more time for silence in our lives, He'll speak to us with fewer interruptions and will fill us with new inspirations, desires, and resolutions. In turn, we can give the fruit of our contemplation to the teens we love.

Biography
Jason Evert has spoken on six continents to more than one million people about the virtue of chastity. He is the author of more than ten books, including *How to Find Your Soulmate without Losing Your Soul*, *Saint John Paul the Great*, and *Theology of the Body for Teens*. Jason earned a master's degree in Theology, and undergraduate degrees in Counseling and Theology, with a minor in Philosophy at Franciscan University of Steubenville. He runs the website chastityproject.com

Find Jason on Social Media:
Twitter.com/jasonevert
Instagram.com/jasonevert
Facebook.com/jasonandcrystalinaevert
Youtube.com/jasonevert

MATT FRADD

What are some of the steps, beyond prayer, that you regularly employ when preparing a talk for teenagers?

Here are three things I'd advise anybody to take seriously before giving a talk:

1. Ask yourself, what is the purpose of this talk? And sum it up in one sentence. If you can't sum it up in one or two sentences, then that may be an indicator you're not clear on the purpose of your talk. For example, one talk I commonly give is called "God, The Universe, and Everything." The purpose of that talk? "To challenge those listening to think deeply about life's deepest questions and help them, using my testimony and arguments, to see the reasonableness of believing in God, Jesus Christ, and the Church He founded."

2. Once you know the purpose of your talk, break your talk into several sections (i.e. prayer, story, testimony, three points to remember, funny slide show, and a challenge). Now examine each section, and ask yourself, how is this section fulfilling the

purpose of my talk? If a section has nothing to do with your main purpose, you may choose to cut it, or if not cut it, reorient it a little so that it does.

3. At the beginning of the talk, articulate to your audience what you're going to tell them. This is nice because it orientates your audience and gives them some idea of where they are, where you're taking them, and what they'll find when they get there. For example, in my Men's talk I say something like this: "There will be two parts to today's talk. In the first half, I would like to simply ask questions and tell stories in order to stir up desire. In the second half, I'd like to suggest five rules that every man must break, if he's to become the man he desires to be, and the man God is commanding him to be."

What are three or four things you tell youth leaders (or try to model for them) to remain conscious of when executing a talk for teens?

1. Don't be someone you're not. Be yourself! As tempting as it might be to steal a joke from Mark Hart, or a visual from Jason Evert, authenticity is key. As my friend Chris Stefanick once said to me, "Dude, just go out there and be your big ol' goofy self." Great advice!

2. Go easy on the self-deprecating humor. Like swearing, self-deprecating humor is a cheap way to get a laugh, but when overused it either discredits you ("If you're that bad, then why are we listening to you?") or makes you look insecure.

3. Instead of using the word "you," "*you* need to realize," etc. Use "us," and "we," "Something *we* constantly need to remind ourselves is... " The latter

is less threatening and usually more humble — we're all in this fight together! The former sounds preachy, and peachiness is always a turn-off.

4. Be careful with how much you move. You don't want to stand stiff as a board because then you'll look uncomfortable, but you don't want to run around the stage like a maniac to avoid seeming uncomfortable because then you'll look (and make everyone else feel) uncomfortable. Don't be afraid to stand in one spot as you make one point, but as you move to the next point, move to a different spot.

How do you evaluate a talk once you've given it? What criteria do you use in deciding if it was as effective as possible or to help you improve in the future?

One way that isn't always helpful is to ask myself, "How well did everyone respond to that? Were they laughing? Crying?" I've given a talk before that, at the time, I didn't think was very good because the crowd was more quiet the usual. Once I got the audio recording, however, I felt it was one of the best talks I had ever given!

One terrifying way to self-evaluate is to videotape your talk. Watch yourself, and on a piece of paper, jot down the positives and the negatives of the way in which you delivered the talk. Ask a trusted friend to be honest with you also. It can hurt to be told, "Dude, you're fly was down!" Or, "Honestly, you were kind of shrill," but you'd much rather know that now than continue being open pant(sed) or ear-piercing.

What has your vast experience speaking to teens taught you over the years? What bit of wisdom would you want to share with youth ministers and Core Members?

Prepare, but don't over prepare. In my experience, while an older more academic audience may want a polished presentation, teens care more about authenticity. Sometimes when we over prepare and deliver it "perfectly," it can come off as rehearsed and insincere.

One of the best pieces of advice I received was "pace yourself." I had this tendency (and probably still do) of beginning my talk in fifth gear — really intense, really animated, and speaking far too quickly. The advice a friend gave me was, "I appreciate your passion, but you've nowhere to go when you want to drive home a point. Relax!" I realized that a real fear of mine was losing the attention of the teens, so I feared to speak normally.

How do you pray before, during, and after a talk? What do you do to ensure it's God on whom you are leaning, and not yourself?

I try to spend a holy hour before the Blessed Sacrament each day that I'm giving talks. I use this time to pray, meditate, and run through my talk in Christ's presence. At the end of every talk I always say "Totus Tuus Maria" three times. My ministry is hers entirely. I figure if what I have to say doesn't end up being effective, it's her fault!

Biography

Matt Fradd works for Covenant Eyes and is the author of the book *Delivered: True Stories of Men and Women Who Turned From Porn to Purity*. A popular speaker and Catholic apologist, he has addressed tens of thousands of people around the world and appeared on EWTN, ABC, and the BBC. Matt is also the founder of this website, ThePornEffect.com, which, if you haven't guessed by now, is dedicated to helping men and women break free from the vice of pornography. He lives in North Georgia, with his wife Cameron and their four children.

Find Matt on Social Media:
Twitter.com/mattfradd
Instagram.com/mattfradd
Facebook.com/mattfradd

BOB RICE

What are some of the steps, beyond prayer, that you regularly employ when preparing a talk for teenagers?

I try to answer the question, "What is the soundbite I want teens to take away from this talk?" At best it's going to be a sentence or a phrase. That gives me a chance to simplify my talk and make it more effective. You can't give a talk on "the Eucharist" in 20 or 30 minutes — it's too huge of a topic. So just focus on one aspect of the Eucharist, like, "the Eucharist is the sacrament of sacraments", or "the Eucharist is the most intimate way we can experience God on earth." I find that most people "over-talk" the subject by trying to include too many things. But, giving a talk focused on one thing they will remember is better than a talk that includes many points that they will forget.

What are three or four things you tell youth leaders (or try to model for them) to remain conscious of when executing a talk for teens?

I emphasize three things to youth leaders when they talk to teens:

1. <u>Scripture.</u> "The Word of God is living and active" (Hebrews 4:12). Whatever you're going to say, God said it better in Scripture. So find those words of God and use them instead of your words. There's more power there!

2. <u>Witness.</u> Blessed Paul VI wrote, "Modern man listens more willingly to witnesses than teachers, and to teachers only if they are witnesses" (*Evangelii Nuntiandi* 41). This doesn't mean you have to give your full testimony every time you give a talk, but you have to give witness as to how you've seen this topic in your life and that you believe in what you are telling them.

3. <u>Relevance.</u> Why should a young person care about this topic? I often ask someone who is preparing a talk, "How does what we say on Sunday night affect what someone does on Monday morning?" We have to show our audience how this message impacts their life. And that means we have to use things in their culture to convey the message effectively.

How do you evaluate a talk once you've given it? What criteria do you use in deciding if it was as effective as possible or to help you improve in the future?

My goal is always to make them cry. If they cried, I did good. If I make a boy cry, I did great. If nobody cried, then I blame whoever led the opening activity.

Seriously though, I go back to that "soundbite." During the social time at the end of the evening, I'd ask teens who had been in the youth group for a while to tell me what the talk was about in one sentence. If they said, "it was about how the Eucharist is the most intimate way to be with God," I know it went well. If they say, "I think it was something about the Eucharist," then I know it wasn't focused enough.

What has your vast experience speaking to teens taught you over the years? What bit of wisdom would you want to share with youth ministers and Core Members?

Always know how you're going to end a talk before you begin it. I've seen a lot of talks ramble on longer than they should have. If you know how you're going to end, it gives you confidence and allows you to make a great presentation. The audience is most likely to remember the last thing you said, so finish strong!

How do you pray before, during, and after a talk? What do you do to ensure it's God on whom you are leaning, and not yourself?

Having Scripture at the heart of the message is what gives me confidence that I'm speaking God's word and not my own. "I am not ashamed of the Gospel: it is the power of God for salvation to every one who has faith" (Romans 1:16). I don't try to be too clever or come up with some new idea. I just want them to more deeply understand God's word and how it applies to their life. When that's the focus, God always speaks to their heart.

Biography
Bob Rice desires to share the love of God using every talent he's been blessed with. He's an internationally known speaker, acclaimed musician, inspirational

teacher, and innovative writer. Bob teaches at Franciscan University of Steubenville, Ohio where he lives with his wife Jennifer and seven beautiful children. You can keep up with him at <u>bob-rice.com</u>.

Find Bob on Social Media:
Twitter.com/therealbobrice

CHRIS STEFANICK

What are some of the steps, beyond prayer, that you regularly employ when preparing a talk for teenagers?

Work! I guess this comes more naturally to some people, but before I hit a "stage" to deliver new material, at minimum, 15 minutes of work went behind every one minute I speak. Sometimes it's an hour behind every minute. I research, write, and practice. I usually make my wife listen! She's great at giving me honest input, always thinking of how I'll be digging deeper into the listener's heart, moving them, and eliciting a response to God.

Then I deliver that talk and note, minute by minute, how the teens responded and what aspects of my presenting I need to tweak to be more effective.

The magic happens when you're really comfortable with a topic, and have learned to be yourself regardless of how big or small the group is that you have the honor of talking to. That might create the illusion that I'm just sharing from the heart, and I am, but I'm never sharing "off the cuff." If you're Mother Teresa, I won't mind you sharing thoughts off the top of your head. Anyone else? Honor your audience by preparing well. Really well. Keep in mind that although some people would rather die than speak to teens, there's a lot of people who would pay to be where you are — sharing your thoughts with a group of listeners. It really is an amazing honor. Treat it like one.

What are three or four things you tell youth leaders (or try to model for them) to remain conscious of when executing a talk for teens?

There are two things you need to be conscious of. First is the truth you're delivering. When I have a really graced experience delivering a talk, I'm "standing under" the truth that I'm delivering. It's far bigger than me. I'm in awe of it.

It's really amazing that God lets us hold these realities in our minds and hearts, and deliver them to others with our mouths. Prophets couldn't have guessed just how awesome the Gospel would be. Angels were in awe as they saw these mysteries unfold. THIS is the stuff we get to deliver.

And we're not just sharing facts, our delivery creates a "space" where the person hearing can encounter God Himself. Our words are just air unless *He* moves in the hearts of the listeners.

The second thing to keep in mind is the teens (or whoever is listening). We have to pray that God shares some of his love for them with us. It can't really be faked. If someone loves the people he's talking to, it shows. If not, then he might be more concerned with how well he's speaking or "performing." And that shows too.

How do you evaluate a talk once you've given it? What criteria do you use in deciding if it was as effective as possible or to help you improve in the future?

My criterion is always the kids. I ask God to show me a glimpse of the impact or lack thereof.

If I get an email after the event or a kid come up to me afterwards sharing how the talk changed him or her, that's confirmation that it was a good talk. And what I'm looking for is change. That someone was brought closer to Christ. I have to be careful not to evaluate the impact in a superficial way. It would be easy, as a speaker, to gauge impact by laughs, or how many kids buy a booklet and ask me to sign it. It would be easy to never *really* challenge kids and sell myself more than the Gospel. And without prayer, we can all fall back into that. I don't care how holy you are. Pride is always a possibility, or call it "self interest." As a speaker who feeds my family in part by the talks I give, the question "will I be invited back?" was one I used to let bug me.

The reality is that sometimes a crowd might be a little stand offish after I speak if I really challenged them, or if the culture at that given school was so broken that a chastity talk not only kicked up a ton of wounds, but made a lot of people (especially the guys who enjoy using girls) really angry – not because I came off like a jerk, but because I (lovingly) got all up in their stuff! But that response can be a good sign that your talk hit the mark too. It was a hit to the gut. Don't expect "high fives" after one of those talks.

And I've gotten good at speaking, in part, because I'm not afraid to objectively judge myself. Speaking is like throwing a football! You have to do it a lot to get good at it, and you have to be unafraid of looking at aspects of your game that just stink. Get input and adjust. It's not about you. I know that's hard because when you speak, in addition to sharing the Gospel, you're kindof ripping your heart out of your chest and showing it to everyone. And "that was okay" or "that wasn't too good" can feel like someone saying, "you're just okay," or "you're not too good." But that's not the case and you have to get over that to improve. I'm still improving. I hope I always do.

What has your vast experience speaking to teens taught you over the years? What bit of wisdom would you want to share with youth ministers and Core Members?

A little youth ministry secret: I give some of the same exact talks to high school freshman as to their parents or even to a group of bishops! Teens don't like being talked down to as if they're "kids." They like begin talked to like they're people. And adults don't like being "theologized" (unless they're part of the .01% of Catholics going for a Theology degree). They like hearing uplifting truths carried by stories and illustrations that they can apply to their lives.

Also, you don't have to be young or cool to impact teens. I'm way more effective with teenagers as a 38-year-old dad than I was as a young 20-something. You just have to be who you are, at whatever phase of life you're in, and love God authentically, and love those kids sincerely.

Then, regardless of how well you speak, you become the message. You become the vessel God uses to make his presence known in the lives of teenagers. And what you're doing is no less important than that! As a Life Teen parish youth minister, I never tried to recruit Core Members with the line "this won't take much of your time." I recruited them by saying "you're gonna change lives."

How do you pray before, during, and after a talk? What do you do to ensure it's God on whom you are leaning, and not yourself?

I got the runs before every talk for my first five years of public speaking. Speaking didn't always come naturally! But I knew I was good at it and called to it. That said, terror was generally something that kept me relying on God.

I'm over that, thank God, or with the amount of speaking I do now I'd have been hospitalized long ago! But I still pray the same. I beg God to anoint my words, to help me speak what those kids need to hear, to help me get over myself and not "perform" a talk but really speak to their hearts, and to help me love them.

In short, I guess you can say I beg God to help me serve Him effectively, and in a way that makes him happy at the same time.

And I used the word "beg" because I pray as if what I'm about to do has the weight of eternal importance attached to it… because it does. Someone's eternal destiny, and the trajectory of their entire lives can be strengthened or changed by the words we speak and the witness we give.

Biography

Chris Stefanick is a co-author and presenter for Chosen. He speaks to more than 50,000 teens, young adults, and parents every year. Chris has served at a parish in the East Los Angeles area and as director of youth and young- adult ministry for the Archdiocese of Denver. He is the founder and president of Real Life Catholic, a nonprofit organization dedicated to reengaging a generation. Chris is a syndicated columnist, has authored or co-authored several books, and is a regular on Catholic TV and radio. Chris and his wife, Natalie, live with their children in Denver, Colorado.

Find Chris on Social Media:
Twitter.com/ChrisStefanick
Facebook.com/reallifecatholic

JOEL STEPANEK

What are some of the steps, beyond prayer, that you regularly employ when preparing a talk for teenagers?

I start preparation by identifying what the focus and purpose of the talk is in relation to the context of the event or retreat. Knowing the purpose of the talk is important for allowing the talk to be what it is meant to be. I think everyone wants to be the person that gives the "home run" talk that teenagers remember, but we often forget that often talks may be set up by several other talks before it, such as the Saturday night retreat talk, or empowerment talk. Think about it this way — a star baseball player can't hit a grand slam unless the three batters before him did their job getting on base.

Once I know the purpose of the talk, I define the focus using one or two sentences. I ask myself, "If a teenager were to tweet about this talk, could they summarize the point in 140 characters or less?" This is important because everything that happens in the talk, as I write and brainstorm, needs to tie back to that focus. It keeps the talk manageable and coherent.

What are three or four things you tell youth leaders (or try to model for them) to remain conscious of when executing a talk for teens?

It is important to be conscious of the three movements of the talk: The takeoff, the takeaway, and the landing. They are the three areas where a good talk turns into a great talk, and where a talk can also completely fail. I always try to *"take off"* with a "power opener," something that catches the audience's attention and makes people lean forward and wonder, "where is he going with this next?" The power opener needs to relate to the talk. You can't just tell a joke that doesn't relate. I never open with, "Thank you, my name is..." That is boring. People hear that all of the time.

The <u>takeaway</u> is what the whole talk focuses around. I write out the message like a thesis statement before the talk. I will always use this statement almost verbatim as I've written it within the talk, and I highlight it with a power pause, a graphic, or repetition. It is the message that people should remember after the talk is done — even if they forget everything else.

The <u>landing</u> is how it all wraps up. I like to tie my landing back to the power opener. It makes the whole talk feel coherent and well executed. This is the place where I challenge the listener to action, prayer and reflection, or discussion. I never end with, "in conclusion," "thank you for listening," or anything that resembles those statements. They feel like hard landings and convey to the audience that you didn't really know how to end the talk.

Finally, I want every talk to lead back to Christ. While I am talking, I want people to be led to Jesus — if a talk isn't leading back to Jesus, then I need to revise it until it is clearly Christocentric.

How do you evaluate a talk once you've given it? What criteria do you use in deciding if it was as effective as possible or to help you improve in the future?

I like to video record my talks on my phone if they aren't being recorded on video. I learned this in High School when I was a wrestler; after meets I would watch film and critique my technique and form. I do the same thing with talks. I count the number of vocal fillers I use such as "um, uh, like," I note places where I lost my train of thought and paused for too long, I rate crowd response to any jokes or anecdotes, and I ask myself if the message was as coherent as I want it to be. Ultimately, I am my toughest critic — and sometimes I am too tough. I am wary of unsolicited compliments after a talk. Sometimes they can hide a mediocre talk because people are just being nice, and other times no one will compliment a great talk because the talk subtly serves only to "set up" the next discussion, dynamic, or talk.

I have a couple of people that I absolutely trust to give me honest feedback to keep my own criticism in check and who will also not sugarcoat a bad talk. In the Church a lot of people say, "great job" because they don't want to hurt my feelings, but the Gospel deserves our very best and I never want my ego to hinder that.

What has your vast experience speaking to teens taught you over the years? What bit of wisdom would you want to share with youth ministers and Core Members?

Watch the technique of great speakers, but keep your personality. I love watching stand-up comedians and learn so much from them because they need to engage an audience for two hours with just a microphone and their voice. I learn so much about how to effectively transition from one topic to another, how to set up a story, and how to read a room. I watch great Catholic speakers and learn how they minister to various groups of teens, the ways they engage a story, and how they present a message. Those are refined techniques – how you get into and out of a talk, how you set up a joke and tie it in, stage presence, how they "takeoff" and "land" a talk – and those are what you emulate and learn from when you observe other speakers.

But remember, you can't emulate personality; be authentic to who you are. Jesus called me to ministry because I bring unique gifts and talents, as well as a unique speaking style. I honor that I am authentic. I can't do, nor should I do, what another speaker does. You won't feel comfortable doing it; it is like going to a dinner party and pretending to be someone else the whole night — totally awkward. Not only that, but teens can smell inauthenticity from a mile away. Your message will only be heard if you are authentic.

How do you pray before, during, and after a talk? What do you do to ensure it's God on whom you are leaning, and not yourself?

I have three stages of prayer before talk: There is initial prayer and brainstorming (prayer storming). I go before the Blessed Sacrament with any talk materials I've been given and I take time to simply offer those up to Christ. I don't write during that time, I just listen. Then, I start to take notes and I write down anything that comes to mind. The Holy Spirit works through a process. A lot of those ideas change but they may be the stepping-stone for another idea and develop into something else. That is the second stage of prayer — refining the talk and leaning on the Holy Spirit. I start writing by asking the Holy Spirit for inspiration, and then I write and work for about an hour or so. I finish, I thank God, and I offer what I've written back up. Finally, on the week of an event, I take notes about everything else that is happening — what words or phrases keep coming up, what other talks are about, any little things that God may be using to help get my attention. I incorporate some of those things in the talk. It is important to note that I rarely, if ever, change my talk entirely based on events of the weekend. That is a lie Satan can use, "your whole talk is wrong - switch it all up." If you are rooted in prayer, the Holy Spirit may bring about some minor tweaks in the talk based on direction, but it is unlikely there will be a major overhaul.

After a talk I thank God for the opportunity to minister, and I offer everything – both good and bad – back to Christ. If glory comes through the talk, that is awesome. If I dropped a bomb, then I trust that God makes up for my human frailty and failing. I will spend time in Adoration thanking God and offering up petitions for all the people that heard the talk, and that the Holy Spirit can work powerfully in their lives.

Biography
Joel Stepanek has been actively and passionately involved in youth ministry for over ten years. What began as a simple internship in a parish youth

ministry office evolved into an incredible adventure that led him on numerous middle school lock-ins, high school retreats, and ultimately to meet his wife, Colleen, who is a campus minister. Together they have son, Elijah Daniel. Joel is the Life Support Coordinator for Life Teen International where he creates engaging youth ministry curriculum for high school students. He loves cooking, reading a great book, and cheers exclusively for the Green Bay Packers.

Find Joel on Social Media:
Twitter.com/LT_Jstepanek

CONCLUSION

If I asked you to list five talks that really have changed your life, you wouldn't be able to. But if I were to ask you to tell me five people that changed your life — you wouldn't be able to narrow it down.

First, be a witness to God's beauty and truth and the words will come. Don't over prepare, and don't under prepare, and don't buy into the lie of what you are not. Know that God has called you and prepared you in advance, and say the words that He has prepared in your heart. And then the greatest gift will come — you will be sitting out there watching them speak to you. And that is awesome.

APPENDIX

The Ten Commandments of Presentation

1. Speak don't read. You'll be easier to understand, and you'll be better able to make genuine contact with your teens.

2. Stand up. You'll be easier to see and hear, and it offers you the authoritative position.

3. Use visual aids. People are visual creatures. Catholicism is an incarnational and sacramental faith. Reinforce words with images when appropriate.

4. Move around. Don't pace but don't stand still. Use your hands and your feet to animate the words coming out of your mouth.

5. Vary the pitch of your voice. Monotones are sleep-inducing. Your voice is your instrument and varying the pitch, tone, and pentameter engages your audience.

6. Speak loudly, clearly, and confidently. Speak from the gut, not the throat. Breathe deeply — it's necessary for volume.

7. Make eye contact with the teens. If eye contact makes you more nervous, stare at foreheads — your audience won't know the difference. Avoid looking at the ground or constantly to the left or to the right half of your audience.

8. Focus on main points. Less is often more. Give them short, striking points that they'll remember. A good rule of thumb is to make no more than three main points in any given talk. Hit those points more than once in different ways.

9. Read body language. If people seem to be disengaged or getting restless or distracted the problem may not be you. Is the room too hot or too cold? Too dark? Can people see you well? Their body posture and silence (or lack thereof) will tell you a great deal.

10. Finish on time. For most teens, the maximum attention span is six-to-ten minutes. If you exceed this limit (unless you are a seasoned presenter to teens), you'll probably lose them.

A Presenter's Checklist

Use this bullet point checklist as you prepare your talk, but prior to giving it:

☐ Have you spent as much time praying for the teens that will hear the talk as you have physically preparing it? Good, now pray some more.

☐ Practice the talk out loud, with full energy in front of another person.

☐ Time yourself.

☐ Record yourself giving the talk to pick up on mannerisms that you do and do not have.

☐ Write down: what in your talk will speak to a

teenager who is coming for the first time.

☐ Write down: what in your talk will speak to a teenager who has been coming for four years.

☐ Write down: one phrase or truth that you want every teen to walk away knowing about this topic. Is the phrase or truth clear or does it get lost in your sharing?

☐ Where are the possible problem areas of your talk?

☐ Is it too deep or "heady"?

☐ Does it have too much information?

☐ Too shallow?

☐ Too much story and not getting to the meat fast enough?

☐ Are you tied to your outline? Do you know it well enough to have a note card with just bullet points and/or key words?

☐ Have you marked your Scripture for quick reference?

☐ Do you have open-ended questions that will derail or cause digression in the talk? (I.e. "Have you guys ever wondered why guys are so hard to figure out?")

☐ Are there any visual aids that can help?

☐ Is a PowerPoint, Keynote, or ProPresenter software presentation necessary for the talk? (If not, then do not use it. PowerPoint presentations need to have a purpose.)

☐ Do you know the talk well enough to cut it down (if

time becomes an issue) without losing the substance?

☐ Do you know what is happening before and after your talk so that you effectively start and end with purpose?

☐ Do you have a timekeeper who will keep you "on time" during your talk without distracting the group?

☐ Do you have an end point that you know well enough to "land the plane," ending your talk with a purpose?

☐ Do you have tangible and relevant examples to challenge the teens to live out the message of your talk that night and the very next morning?

☐ Does your talk tie back into devotional prayer (Sacraments, Scripture, personal prayer time, a physical encounter of Jesus Christ) and not you?